NEVER KISS
A
TURTLE

To JoAnn
and Arthur,

Warm wishes,

Nancy Clapton Myles

NEVER KISS A TURTLE

NANCY CLOPTON MYERS

Illustrated by Elaine Gill Claiborne

iUniverse, Inc.
New York Bloomington

NEVER KISS A TURTLE
The Joys and Sorrows of Pet Ownership

iUniverse books may be ordered through booksellers or by contacting:
iUniverse
1663 Liberty Drive
Bloomington, IN 47403
www.iuniverse.com
1-800-Authors (1-800-288-4677)

ISBN: 978-1-4502-4838-9 (pbk)
ISBN: 978-1-4502-4839-6 (ebk)

Printed in the United States of America
iUniverse rev. date: 9/8/10

TABLE OF CONTENTS

INDEX OF FOUR-FOOTED FRIENDS

CANINES

FELINES

POUNCER   Cream Tabby 1991-2003

PICKLE   Black Striped 2004

CUDDLES   Tortoiseshell 2004-

RODENT

BIFF   Gerbil 1987-88

RABBITS

HOPPITY 1,2 & 3   Domestic White 1966-67

PREFACE

In my seventy plus years, I have never been without at least one pet in my life. In fact, according to my mother, my first sentence was "Go 'way, Mitzi" (a Manchester terrier.) I feel strongly about the benefits of taking a helpless animal into your home and making him or her part of the family. Not only does it teach compassion and responsibility to a child, it also provides hours of amusement and companionship.

In nearly 50 years of marriage, my husband and I owned a parade of animals, and it seems we were always having unusual or amusing experiences related to the pets. Over time, I regaled my bridge foursome with stories, and so when I retired and mentioned that I needed a project, they suggested I put some of my tales in writing. The title comes from their favorite story of Schnitz and the turtle.

Every incident in the book is absolutely true and is recounted to the best of my memory. The human characters you'll meet include my opinionated husband, Larry, and our children Eric and his younger (by 4 1/2 years) sister, Mindy. The book is dedicated to them, with whom I shared all these experiences and to the animals themselves.

I spent two years in writing this work, interrupted by the sudden death of my husband. It's been a fun but poignant journey for me. My only regret is that the only other person, who knew all these pets and would have enjoyed this book the most, will never read it.

IN MEMORY OF
LAWRENCE E. MYERS
1937 - 2008

ACKNOWLEDGEMENTS

First, I want to thank my longtime friends Julie, Joyce and Donelea who suggested the idea of a book and then encouraged me through the process.

Next, thanks to my good friend Elaine Claiborne who provided the clever illustrations and followed my progress on nearly a day-to-day basis.

I'm grateful to Joyce Whitehead for her photography expertise in readying some very old photos for use in the book.

My children, Eric Myers and Mindy Allen, were helpful in remembering details, and Mindy often provided "tech support" for my limited computer skills.

And lastly, I offer a kudo for my editor, Debbie Freeman, who so capably and quickly went over the manuscript for me.

1. OUR FIRST PET

When a couple marries, each brings to the union preconceived ideas and traditions from his or her birth family. Fortunately, when my husband, Larry, and I married in 1960, we both had been raised with pets as an integral part of our lives. The only difference was my pets (dogs and cats) had been indoor animals, whereas Larry was used to hunting dogs that lived in a pen outside. Thus, it took a little convincing on my part to get him to agree to a dog in the house, or in our case, a three-room apartment. I have to admit, the convincing was easier then when I was still a bride and he was still very eager to please me!

Actually, a pet was not part of our game plan at that time. We were living in Norfolk, Virginia, where Larry was stationed with the Navy. I should say I was living there and Larry was there only when the ship was in port.

His duties with the Navy led to long cruises and therefore loneliness for me and the need for companionship, and ultimately, the somewhat irrational decision to get a dog. A dog would provide a "lot of company" and an inexpensive burglar alarm!

So it was that one Saturday afternoon, we set out to the local pound, and after paying the appropriate fees (remembering our financial straits, it surely couldn't have been more than $5) and filling out papers, we headed home with some sort of black-and-white terrier. We named her "Mo" after our home state of Missouri and joked that she was our first child. We learned two things immediately: (1) Mo was not housetrained and showed little interest in the whole process, and (2) she didn't appear to be too intelligent.

Our "furnished" apartment (and that's using the term loosely) had white shag rugs, except that the shag had pretty much worn off, so it was like a white canvas on the floor. Mo would come flying up the stairs, in the door and hit the rug with all four feet. Then she'd apply the "brakes" and slide the entire 12-foot width of the living room, dragging the rug with her. It became a great game for her, and she loved watching me straighten it back out.

Mo did fulfill her watchdog duties. One very warm night, when I had the bedroom windows open to get relief from the humid Norfolk summer, Mo started barking frantically. I yelled at her to be quiet, and then I heard a voice from across the street say, "Get away from there!" The next morning the neighbor called to tell me he had seen a man looking in my window. It was a very frightening experience for me, and in spite of my "watch dog," we moved to a second-floor apartment.

Three Mo stories remain in my memory. The first has to do with the very traumatic experience of baking my first pie. I love lemon meringue pie, so armed with my Better Homes & Gardens cookbook and a lot of confidence, I began. The first challenge was the crust. After trying several times to roll it out and get it into a pie pan, I ended up with a sticky mass. I solicited the help of the older (by all of 5 years) lady who lived upstairs. We finally mastered it and I started on the lemon filling, cooking it according to directions. So far, so good! Now, it's time for the meringue.

Just "beat three egg whites until they stand in peaks and add sugar." How difficult can that be, especially with my new wedding-gift mixer? After trying three times and holding that "lightweight" portable appliance until my arm felt as if it might come loose at the shoulder any moment, I decided to call my mother back in Missouri. This was a major decision because I didn't want her to know her new college graduate couldn't decipher a simple recipe; and secondly, a long-distance call was definitely not in our budget! But since I was running out of options, I did it. Her first question was, "Did you get any yolk in the egg whites?" My tearful response was, "I don't know; does that make a difference?" It does!

Anyway, I used my last three eggs, tried once more and surprise! It worked! It actually looked like a beautiful lemon-meringue pie, and I felt a surge of domestic pride. Never mind the fact that I had spent nearly five hours making it! I carefully carried it to the dining room table and sat down to rest until it was time to go pick up Larry from the ship. Then, in my peripheral vision, I saw Mo walking into the room, licking her chops! NO! It couldn't

be! But it was. She had climbed onto a chair, then on to the table where she licked every bit of meringue from the pie! I was still crying when I got to the ship, and Larry said, "It's okay; you can just make another one!" Actually, to this day, I still have not made another lemon meringue pie!

The second Mo story was a prank on Larry. To his dying day, he insisted that it was deliberate, as if Mo were smart enough to plan something like this. Larry's commanding officer had scheduled a full dress inspection for the next day. Being a junior officer, my husband was always very conscientious about these. I had starched, sprinkled and ironed his shirt and cap cover until they were perfect. He had stretched the cover over the cap and secured it tightly and then polished all the brass buttons and his belt buckle. Then he had carefully laid everything out for the morning, placing his hat on the bedroom chair.

When we awakened, there was an unmistakable odor in the bedroom and sure enough, Mo had climbed onto the chair during the night and used Larry's immaculate white cap cover for her toilet! The cap was brown and the Ensign's language was blue! I'm certain everyone in the eight-plex apartment could hear him. We never quite figured out how she managed to position herself to accomplish this feat, and if I hadn't seen it myself, I'm sure I wouldn't believe it!

Fall came and with it the start of my teaching assignment, which meant that Mo was alone all day in the apartment. Fearing what she might find to entertain herself, we confined her to the bathroom, which was the only place with a lock where she couldn't get into any trouble. WE THOUGHT!

The first day, she shredded two rolls of toilet paper. It looked as if a gerbil had made a nest. (That might have been a better choice for a pet?)

The next day, I removed all paper products from the bathroom so she ate a tube of toothpaste. I didn't realize this until I tried to brush my teeth and toothpaste came out of 10 different holes! "She's bored," I told myself. Trying my best to be patient, the next day I removed the toilet paper and toothpaste and thoughtfully left her toys and a water dish in the bathroom. That day, she chewed two new bath towels and a washcloth!

The next day, I announced in each of my classes that I was looking for a home for a cute terrier puppy. She likes children and would love a big yard to play in. Sure enough, one of my students came in the following day and said her family would like to have Mo. After a phone call to her parents to confirm the arrangement, Mo went with me to school the next day and I dropped her off at her new home. I have to admit, it was NOT a difficult decision!

2. A NEW PUPPY

Two years had passed since our first experience with pet ownership and if we learned anything from Mo, it was not to have a dog in an apartment. We were back in our hometown of Kansas City, and with a check from the government for unused leave time, we had purchased our first actual house! Correction: We put a down payment on our first house and have moved in! It was a four-room post-war (that's World War II) bungalow in Prairie Village, a young community on the Kansas side of the two-state metropolitan area. The big selling point to us was that a large family room had been added to the back of the house, AND the backyard was fenced. This meant it was time for, hopefully, a more permanent pet.

My last childhood dog had been a cocker spaniel and my parents now owned a Chihuahua, and Larry's family still had Mike, a German shorthaired pointer. Mike was a hunting dog and lived in the backyard in a dog run. He was only allowed in the house for short visits. That was not my idea of a "pet." So the debate was on! What kind of dog should we get?

We had recently visited some high-school friends who had a male dachshund named Ernie. Our host placed Ernie's favorite toy atop a door, teasing the poor sad-eyed little dog. Ernie sat and stared at the ball as if he were studying the situation and trying his best to figure out a way to retrieve it. He tried jumping, but it didn't take long to decide that his seven-inch height was no match for a seven foot door! After at least 20 minutes of whining and staring at the ball, he suddenly lunged against the door, slamming it shut and of course, the ball fell off. Ernie grabbed it and ran to parts unknown, probably to hide it from those mean humans!

Larry laughed and was very impressed with the tenacity of this little 12-pound dog. I think his exact words were, "He's as stubborn a German as I am!" (I must tell you there's still room for debate there.) We did agree that he was not only cute, but determined and smart, so the decision was made: When we had a house, it was to be a dachshund for us!

Any experienced dog trainer will tell you that at least in the Midwest, it's best to get a puppy in the springtime, so that you can train him to go outside immediately.

We moved into our house on December 21, 1962, and on the 23rd, we brought home our adorable miniature dachshund. His name had to sound German, of course, and we settled on Schnitzel (as in wiener schnitzel.) Neither of us had ever eaten wiener schnitzel or even knew exactly what it was, but it sounded good. One problem: The AKC already had a dachshund by that name, so we had to vary it somehow. We decided on Baron von Schnitzel, a rather pompous title for this cute little guy. So, it was immediately shortened to Schnitz or Schnitzy. We didn't know it at the time, but this was the beginning of a 16-year love affair with this loyal friend and a 40-year association with the breed.

He was only six weeks old, newly weaned, and missed his mother terribly. We purchased baby blankets and stuffed animals from a nearby garage sale, and arranged them in an empty Budweiser box and then placed it strategically next to our own bed. If, or rather, when, he cried, we could reach down and pat him. None of the three of us got much sleep the first few nights. Incidentally, the term "box" for "bed" stuck and fifteen years later, we were still commanding him to "Get in your box!" For four days, we held him and played with him and fussed over him, until suddenly, the party was over! Christmas vacation had ended, and it was time for us to go back to work!

3. A SAFE PLACE FOR SCHNITZ

Our basement was divided into two rooms and since one was virtually empty, we decided that this would be a great place for Schnitz to stay while we were gone. The only problem was the stairs. He was too small to climb them, and since they were open, he could easily fall off and hurt himself on the concrete floor. Larry found a window screen that wasn't being used, and secured it at the foot of the stairs to form a barricade.

This worked for two days, and on the third, we opened the front door and heard him crying. He sounded surprisingly close, and sure enough, he was at the top of the basement stairs, waiting for us! He had chewed through the screen wire, a hole just large enough to squeeze his small body through. It must have taken him most of the day, and we were concerned that he might have ingested some of the metal! This apparently was not the case, or else he had a very strong stomach, because he suffered no ill effects. There's that determination we so admired in our friends' Ernie. Be careful what you ask for!

Back to square one! We still didn't have a safe place for Schnitz. Obviously, the stairs were still too dangerous, so we had to confine him in the kitchen and family room which had vinyl floors, rather than carpet (and a new carpet at that!) The only barricade big enough and strong enough to close it off was our kitchen table; so every morning, before leaving for work, we cleared the table, turned it onto its side and blocked the door. This worked well for about a week, until one night we unlocked the door and there was Schnitz, waiting in the entry hall to greet us, tail wagging, brown eyes looking up at us as if to say, "Look what I did; aren't you proud of me?" What he had done was to nose the table or jump at it until it moved enough for him to squeeze through. This little dog was not only smart, he was strong!

4. EDUCATING SCHNITZ

As I recall, Schnitz was fairly easy to potty train, especially considering it was winter in Kansas! Of course, we did have to shovel a path to and around the tree in the front yard. After all, his legs were only four inches long and the snow was at least that deep, so you can visualize which part of him was dragging in the snow!

Since this was our first "child" and apparently we didn't have enough to do, we spent a lot of time in teaching the dog wonderful tricks to entertain our friends. He really did learn to count to three, but beyond that, it was simply following hand signals and knowing he would get a special treat if he did it correctly. He could "multiply," do "cube root" and all simple two-digit math addition and subtraction. I can still hear them practicing late into the night with the dog barking, and Larry yelling, "No, I said, two!"

As long as Larry held his treat, Schnitz would bark. When the master's hand dropped slightly, he stopped barking, so as long as the trainer knew the answer, he would get it right. It's amazing that normally intelligent people didn't catch on to the trick, but they didn't. One exception was our good friend Bonnie, who watched the demonstration and said, "Shoot, if you hold that meat long enough, he'd keep barking all night!"

Word spread about his amazing math prowess. I was working at the NBC affiliate in Kansas City then, and when it came time to celebrate "National Dog Week," they were searching for a recording of dogs barking. One of my co-workers suggested that they just have me bring Schnitz in to the studio. I was concerned that he wouldn't perform for me as well as he did for his more forceful masculine trainer, but I agreed to try. I brought him down one evening, after hours, for his recording session. The engineer placed him on a table in front of a microphone and I held the treat above his head. He barked on command, counted and did math problems. They replayed it all week on the air. As we were leaving the building, I stopped for a drink at the water cooler, and Schnitz broke away from me. To my horror, he ran onto the set while they were broadcasting the Ten

O'clock News. One of the stage hands retrieved him but not before he got on camera. I still think he should have gotten a talent fee!

Schnitz learned to sit up; even though we never encouraged this because we were told it was hard on his long back. None the less, he would sit for long periods of time at the front window in our living room. It was low enough that he could just see out and watch for other canine friends and cars driving by.

He was also taught to "STAY" with his "HEAD DOWN," and even when tempted with a piece of meat in front of his nose, he wouldn't move. Finally, after what must have seemed like an eternity to him, he was told, "Okay, you can have it." People always sympathized with the dog and said we were mean, but Schnitz knew he would get it eventually.

5. THE PEEPING SCHNITZ

In those days, we took our canine son with us anywhere we possibly could and some places we probably shouldn't have. Not that he was spoiled, but after leaving him alone all week while we worked, we certainly didn't want him to be lonesome on the weekends. We would wait for a movie to hit the drive-in, so Schnitz could go with us.

One Saturday, after crying through "Days of Wine and Roses," I used the intermission to take Schnitz for a potty break. When it was my turn, I took him into the ladies room with me (on a leash, of course) and ultimately into the stall. I was taught by my germ-cautious Mother to always "assume the stance" in public restrooms, and while I was in that compromising position, I heard a high pitched shriek from the next stall.

When I looked down, there was Schnitz, sticking his long brown nose under the partition. I don't even want to know what he was trying to do to the unsuspecting woman next to me. I  remained in the locked stall until I was certain everyone else had left the premises.

6. CUSTOM MADE DOG CLOTHES

The first year passed, and as the days grew longer and temperatures fell, we learned a harsh truth: this short-haired, cold-blooded breed definitely was not suited to Kansas winters. Poor Schnitz was cold all the time, indoors and out, and shivered constantly. We went shopping for a dog sweater, and found out that he was impossible to fit!

If we bought a "small", which the tag indicated was the correct size for his 12-pound weight, it fit fine around the neck, stretched over his barrel chest, and then stopped halfway down his back! The legs of the sweater dragged the ground, because his legs were so short, and he nearly tripped on it. Some evenings, he would completely slip his legs out of the sweater legs and just lay like a big lump on my lap, warm, but totally unable to walk!

So I decided the only solution to Schnitzel's sartorial problem was for me to use my minimal sewing skills and tailor him a coat. I purchased washable wool, and after carefully measuring his long body, I made a pattern and cut two long pieces of fabric. I fashioned a collar, which buttoned around his neck, and then two straps with more buttons, to hold the coat in place. It was long enough to extend the length of his back to the tail. The only problem was that the second strap hit him in a very vulnerable spot. Apparently, being warm was more important to him than being comfortable because he didn't object. Good

thing I chose a washable fabric though because more than once, it got wet!

As Christmas approached, I was on maternity leave, awaiting the imminent birth of our first child. Desperate for a project, I made the dog a stocking to match ours, and then a red Santa suit, so that he would be properly attired for the holiday. Then we took him to visit our good friends, Alex and Linda. We had him sit up at their door while we hid in the bushes and then instructed him to bark. He was a great hit! We all laughed at our little Santa Dog!

7. THE "BIG BROTHER"

Our human son was born shortly after Schnitzel's first birthday (7th in dog years) and even though he was displaced as our only child, the dog handled it surprisingly well. The first time the baby cried, he rushed into the nursery, sat up by the bassinet and cocked his head, as if to say, "What's that strange noise?"

As Eric grew, they became the best of pals, even though the rambunctious toddler put him in the toy box, chased him in his walker and grabbed him in inappropriate places! I think Schnitz thought all the dropped food on the floor made it worthwhile!

8. THE NEIGHBORHOOD STUD

Schnitz became the ultimate canine lover and the blame should probably rest with his owners. We decided, early on, that he was so remarkable that we'd like to breed him and share his virtues with the world! We registered him with our vet and even advertised in the paper. Soon the stud service was up and running. He was in great demand because even though his papers said he was a "standard" dachshund, he was smaller than most males and therefore less intimidating to the shy female. Larry loved to tell the story of the time they had to get a box for him to stand on in order to reach the object of his affection! Then she dragged him across the floor to get to her water dish. That had to hurt!

Once the owner of the female wanted him to stay several days at their home, but Larry assured him that one hour would be sufficient. It was! He never missed. We bred him enough that he easily earned his keep in stud fees. The only problem was, we created a monster. Apparently, once he had a taste of the opposite sex, he liked it, because more than once, he went out looking for love! When we moved to Overland Park, there was a leash law and we didn't have a fenced yard. Schnitz had a route he would travel each morning, visiting his girl friends. If one of them happened to be in heat, he would

camp on her doorstep, crying. He (or rather, his master) was ticketed twice, and once, he (the dog) was taken by the dog catcher. Eventually, we decided it was cheaper to buy a fence than to continue bailing him out!

9. DON'T FENCE ME IN!

Schnitzel really enjoyed his morning routine of "running his traps" as we called it, so when the new fence was installed, he was not a happy camper! Each day, he went to the front door to be let out, and when we took him to the back door instead, he had to be convinced to venture out at all. It didn't take long for him to find escape routes. We'd put him in the fenced backyard and when he was ready to come in, we'd find him innocently sitting at the front door, looking up as if to say, "fooled you again!"

Remember that Schnitz's owner was as determined as the dog, so every night he would do a walking inspection of the yard's perimeter, plugging up any holes he found. He started with dirt fill, then rocks and finally, he poured concrete in strategic digging places! This worked for a week or so, until Schnitz showed up at the front door again! Larry put him out, then stealthily followed him to discover his new escape route. Sure enough, on the side of the house, out of view, he had dug yet another hole!

We plugged it with a brick and then let the dog out to see what he would do. He waited quietly for the door to close, and then made a beeline for his "spot." When it came into view, he stopped short and stared in disbelief. It didn't take a lot of imagination to see what he was thinking. Then he approached slowly, lifted his leg and thoroughly saturated the offending brick. Could it be that our now teen age (in dog years) son has developed a bit of attitude?

10. THE ACCIDENTAL LITTER

One hot summer day, Larry was up on a ladder painting the house (a one-time thing, incidentally) when a neighbor from several doors down walked into the yard and introduced himself. As Schnitz looked innocently on, he asked, "Is this your dog?" Seems he had a female dachshund and our Schnitz was about to become a father! All the larger dogs had tried to jump over his fence, but Schnitz dug under! OOPS!

To register the litter, he needed our signature. Any paternity doubt we may have had vanished when the puppies were born. They all looked exactly like Schnitz despite the fact that their mother was black and tan. Larry commented that he felt he was paid for rape!

Schnitzel's interest in the opposite sex wasn't limited to canines. He was especially fond of my good friend Donelea. Whenever she came to visit, as soon as she sat down, he would jump on her lap. In the summer, she often wore low-cut blouses and he would stick his long nose in her cleavage, content to stay there as long as she'd allow it. At first it was embarrassing, but then it became a joke that his girlfriend was here! Fortunately, Donelea likes dogs!

11. THE ETERNAL OPTIMIST

Years later when Schnitz was 13 (91 in dog years!) we were playing cards with neighbors at our kitchen table one Saturday night when we heard the dog at the front door. We had long since given up on keeping him confined and figured at his advanced age, he wouldn't go far or get into too much trouble. Surely his "cruising days" were over. Little did we know!

When I opened the door, he limped in, dripping blood all over the entry hall. He had a nickel-sized hole in his right ear and you could actually see light through it! I called our vet at home and he agreed to meet me at the office even though it was after hours.

In the meantime, we found out the true story. There was a female Doberman down the street who was in heat, and her owner told us that Schnitz had dug under the fence (again!) and tried to make friends with her. In rejecting his advances, she bit him! The doctor put 10 stitches in his ear and marveled at his chutzpah. As I recall, his exact words were "I hope I have that much optimism at his age!"

12. THIS LITTLE DOGGY WENT TO MARKET

Schnitz loved to ride in the car, especially our second car, a 1959 VW bug. To provide a little background, this car presented more than a few challenges. In fact, I often said my biggest accomplishment in my job was just getting there. In the winter, I had to park the car around the corner on a hill, so that I could let it roll, pop the clutch and jump-start it every morning. Otherwise, I couldn't get it out of the garage.

The car had no gas gauge. You simply drove it until it ran out of fuel and then there was a lever on the floorboard to kick which switched to a one gallon auxiliary tank. Invariably, this happened on the interstate. The car would suddenly slow to a crawl, traffic flying by on both sides and horns blaring angrily, while I was frantically kicking with my left foot to find the extra gas. It's still a wonder to me that my little blue bug wasn't squashed by an impatient semi.

Another unique feature to the car was the "wind wings." These were triangular shaped little windows on each side that opened independently of the larger roll-down windows. Schnitz loved to stick his long nose out the small opening and breath in the fresh air, no matter how cold it was. There were no locks on the wind wings. You simply pulled them shut and they closed fairly securely unless you were a determined dachshund with a small girth!

One day I was in the supermarket, pushing Eric in the cart and collecting the week's groceries, when my child started pointing and laughing. When I turned to look, here came Schnitz strolling out from behind the meat counter, nose to the ground, searching for any dropped morsels. Who knows how long he'd been there! Apparently he was close enough to the floor that he hadn't attracted any attention. I scooped him up, grabbed Eric under the other arm and trying

to be as inconspicuous as possible, I fled the store, leaving cart, groceries and all!

When we got to the car, I saw that he had nosed open the wind wing, squeezed his small long body through the opening dropped four feet to the ground and ran into the store as an unsuspecting customer entered. Talk about resource-fulness.

13. THE RELUCTANT PAPER BOY

One of the tricks that Larry taught Schnitz was to fetch. He would bring nearly anything if asked by his master to do so. We had a tri-level house at this time, and once I yelled upstairs for Larry to bring my cough medicine when he came downstairs. A few moments passed and I heard the command, "Take this to Mom!" and Schnitz came flying down two flights of stairs, ears standing straight out, with a bottle of cough medicine clutched tightly in his mouth.

Perhaps his most useful trick was fetching the daily newspaper. Every morning, without complaint, he would run out, grab the paper and bring it to the door. Granted, he occasionally took a quick potty stop at the oak tree.

I'm sure he hated Sundays, because the paper was three times bigger than usual and possibly outweighed him. On these days, he sometimes had to grab the string tying the paper and drag it up the driveway. Finally on a wintry Sunday morning, when the snow was as high as his back,  he rebelled. He'd finally had it with this master who demanded the impossible! After hopping in the snow for a few feet, looking for all the world like a brown rabbit, he would pause and look mournfully back at the door. "Do I have to?"

Larry would encourage him and finally, he made it down the driveway to the paper at which time he turned, looked back one last time and then raised his leg. Very systematically he wet the paper from one end to the other. The message was clear! After retrieving the paper by human hands and drying it with the hair dryer, we never sent him out again in the snow without first shoveling a path.

14. NEVER KISS A TURTLE

In 1968, Eric and Schnitz acquired a baby sister. They both accepted her easily into the family routine, in part because she was a sweet, quiet baby and in part because they had no choice!

Any time we happened to be driving on a rural road and spotted a box turtle crawling along, Eric would clamor to stop and rescue him. Often we'd take them home to live in a cardboard box and feast on lettuce and other assorted vegetables. Eric named one of them "Walter Cronkite" and he was in residence several months.

So it was not unusual when we brought home yet another turtle, but this one seemed especially active. He moved around more than his predecessors and kept turning over the box. Several friends advised me that it was beneficial to have a turtle on patrol in the basement to eat any insects that might be down there. I quit worrying about him and in truth, forgot that he was there at all!

One evening, Larry was on a sales call and I was working in the basement with the children and of course, Schnitz, nearby. The phone rang and I was talking with my mother when suddenly, the dog yelped in obvious pain. I turned to look and to my horror, I saw Schnitz' pink tongue was hanging out of his mouth at least 5 inches and attached to the other end was the turtle!

Assessing the situation, I could see that his shell was clamped tightly shut with the dog's tongue caught inside. I grabbed the dog in one hand and the turtle in the other. If I tried to let go of either, the dog wriggled and his tongue was pulled out even further! Like an idiot, I screamed, "Let go!" He didn't. The baby was crying, Schnitz was whining in terror, Eric (now age five) was running in circles, and all the while, my poor mother is hearing all this over the phone line.

It's a family joke that mother always knew what to do in any situation, so having no ideas of my own, I instructed Eric to pick up the phone, tell her what was happening and ask her what we should do. After relaying all this to his grandmother, Eric turned and said, "Granny says, 'Kill the damn thing.'" My mother was a gentle woman, raised a Southern Baptist, and she rarely used bad language, and I'd never known her to resort to violence; but desperate times call for desperate measures!

While still clutching both animals, I sent Eric to bring me the hammer. After what seemed an eternity, he reappeared and said, "I couldn't find the hammer, Mommy, but here's a "screwderator." I brought it down as hard as possible on the terrapin's back and at last, he released his prey.

I told Eric to "throw" the turtle out the back door, but having been taught to be kind to animals, he just released him and told him to "shoo." I didn't even look at the turtle; my concern was whether the dog could ever chew again. He was walking around slowly sticking his tongue in and out as if to be sure it still functioned. I gave him water and after reporting to Granny on the phone, I placed a call to our college friend who was now a practicing veterinarian. When he could stop laughing long enough to talk, he assured me that if there were no cuts and he was eating and drinking, he'd be okay.

The kicker to this (which is my favorite Schnitz story) is that the following week at my neighborhood bridge club, one of the ladies told of her children finding a poor box turtle whose shell was broken. She said it looked as if someone had just hit it with a hammer! "Who would do such a thing?" she cried indignantly! Silently, I'm thinking "It wasn't a hammer; it was a screwdriver!"

Some 35 years later, Eric told this story at his grandmother's funeral as an example of how Granny always knew how to handle any domestic situation. I should point out that Granny was raised on a farm and did not believe that wild animals (including turtles) should ever be allowed in the house or basement! It was then I decided that my mother was a very wise woman, and after this incident, no turtles were ever allowed in our house or basement either!

15. SCHNITZ THE PATHFINDER

When the family went camping, Schnitz went along, sharing a sleeping bag with one of the kids and even going out in the boat with us. We weren't sure of his swimming skills, so Larry threw him in the lake to test them. The theory was "all dogs can swim" and he did, although he looked a little wide-eyed and did a furious dog paddle to the shore.

Once, in his later years, we were at Lake Stockton in the Missouri Ozarks and he wandered away from the campsite. We never quite established blame; both adults thought the other was in charge of the dog.

At any rate, I took the car and started off to look for him, while the rest of the family searched the woods. He was old; he had cataracts and his hearing wasn't too good.

There were lots of larger dogs, snakes and other predators around there. We were all worried!

After a frantic hour's search (it seemed much longer), I drove the half mile to the Son Sac Motel where Larry's parents were staying to give them the bad news.

I pulled up in front of eight identical doors, and there, sitting in front of #4 was our little lost dog! Of course, that was the unit the folks were in! We never quite figured out how he knew. Did he remember visiting them the night before? Was it smell or just instinct? Or was he really that smart? It didn't matter. It was a very joyful reunion, filled with doggy kisses and human tears!

16. THE SURPRISE PET

My father-in-law was a raucous, soft-hearted German who loved his first grandchild fiercely! I'm sure it never occurred to him to check with the parents before buying a new pet for the boy, so one day he showed up at the door with a fluffy white rabbit! Naturally, Eric loved it, and promptly christened him "Hoppity." Daddy then spent four hours building a hutch to house the newest critter. It was a very sturdy cage, but no one mentioned that he should have put a shield of some sort around the bottom. We soon learned that rabbits make lots of little "raisins" as Eric called them, and Hoppity liked to kick them out of the cage.

He took up residence in a corner of the family room; then he was relegated to the garage and eventually to the backyard. It was there that, unfortunately, he met his demise when some cruel neighborhood teenagers pinned him with a tomato stake! Of course, Eric was broken-hearted, so we immediately went to the pet store and bought a new Hoppity!

This one somehow escaped from his cage and decided to hop the neighborhood one day. I quickly learned that rabbits don't come when they're called! I cornered him under some shrubs about a block from our house.

The next crisis occurred shortly afterward when Eric took him out of his hutch to play on the basement floor. (Hoppity II had been moved to the basement after the backyard tragedy!) We allowed short periods of freedom as long as someone was watching him.

However, with a four-year-old attention span, Eric soon forgot Hoppity and ran on to something new. My first indication of trouble came when I heard a high-pitched wail. I never knew rabbits had a sound, but I discovered what it meant when I raced to the basement and found Schnitz carrying a very dead rabbit!

When I called Larry at the office to report this latest fatality, I lobbied to just explain to Eric that this was the dog's nature. Schnitz didn't mean to hurt the bunny; it was just survival of the fittest. I didn't want the child to hate the dog for destroying his other pet. We needed to be honest, responsible parents. We should NOT, under any circumstances, consider replacing the rabbit!

When Larry was a little late in arriving home, I suspected that he had ignored my opinion. You see, he was a soft-hearted German like his father. When he sneaked into the basement with a vented pet carrier, it could mean only one thing: Hoppity III!

The only problem was this one had a small black spot on his back. Eric immediately noticed it and we told him Hoppity must have gotten dirty in the basement! So much for honesty in parenting!

17. SCHNITZ THE BIRD DOG

I mentioned that Larry's father always owned a bird dog and hunting was a tradition in their family. Rather than invest in an expensive pointer of some sort, Larry decided to train Schnitz. After all, dachshunds were originally bred to hunt badgers, so it was part of his heritage! That's why he had the large barrel chest to dig down into the den. Also, he was very smart and extremely loyal to Larry, AND he had a keen nose. Why not train him to flush out quail coveys? Since he would fetch anything from newspapers to balls, why not a bird?

After several dry runs and practice using a quail wing and pheasant feathers, Schnitz was ready for his debut. The family made its annual Thanksgiving Day trek to Uncle Jack's farm near Atchison, and after dinner, Larry and his brother Bill set out with an eager little brown dog ranging in front of them searching for quail.

They were gone less than an hour when we spotted them coming back across the field. Bill was carrying both guns and the ammo pouch, and Larry was carrying the dog! It seems his legs were not long enough to lift him above the stubble in the field and his poor tummy was scratched and bleeding! His humans had failed to take into account the difference between practicing on a manicured lawn and actually running in the field. Thus ended Schnitzel's career as the "world's smallest bird dog!"

18. CHESTER THE POINTER

This explains why Larry decided to get an actual hunting dog, thinking it would make all the difference in his hunting success. (It didn't.) We named the dog Chester, in honor of one of Larry's dad's drinking buddies. He was a registered German short-haired pointer. To share the expense of installing a backyard dog run, Larry convinced a neighbor to buy Chester's litter mate, Count. We split expenses and the idea was our children would share the cleaning duties as part of their household chores. (As I recall, this plan wasn't too successful!)

We had a special disposal built into the run, with chemicals to dissolve the waste. I don't know how effective it was, because in warm weather, there was a definite aroma.

We got Chester as a pup, and after a year, it was time for him to go to bird dog school so he'd be trained in time for hunting season in the fall. We drove him 100 miles south to a trainer who had been highly recommended. After one week of a three-week program, we got a phone call asking us to pick him up. The trainer said he was just "not ready" for college yet. We could try again when he was more mature.

Larry drove down to get him, and when the dog spotted his master, he got so excited that he jumped out of the elevated kennel and broke his leg! The vet set his leg and put a cast on it. He presented us with a large bill and the assurance that he would be "good as ever."

As it turned out, this was not the case. A hunting dog with a limp is not of much use in the field. Since we already had a pet, we decided to sell him to recoup some of the expense we'd had. The man who bought him was thrilled to get a registered German short-hair; he

didn't mind the altered gait. The last we heard, Chester was living in his garage and had chewed through all the cords on his power tools! Guess the trainer was right; he was immature!

19. THE LITTLE GENERAL

The years passed quickly in our busy household. Schnitz was getting too old to play with the children, and we could see his days were numbered, so we decided to buy another miniature dachshund, thinking it might ease the pain when Schnitz was gone. This one was black and tan and he was a gift for Eric's 12th birthday.

Even at that young age, our son was a history buff, and especially studied World War II, so searching for a strong German name for his new puppy, he chose "Rommel" after the Nazi General. All dachshunds are cold blooded, but Rommel figured out a unique way to deal with the problem. Since our family room was on the lower level and therefore colder than the rest of the house, we had daily fires in the fireplace.

Rommel would sit on the raised hearth and bask in the warmth of the fire; then he discovered that the residue ashes were very warm, so he'd crawl into the fireplace and bury himself! It took us a while to figure out why he always seemed to have grey dust on his black coat!

Unfortunately, Rommel had a congenital kidney defect and lived less than a year. His young master felt responsible and was sure he hadn't kept his water dish full. It was one of those sad experiences that you wish you could spare your child.

20. RASCAL

After losing Rommel suddenly, we had a mixed terrier named "Rascal." I met her at a Tupperware party among a litter of puppies who desperately needed homes. I've always been a pushover for soft brown eyes, and I couldn't stop thinking about her. I took the family out to see her the next day, and of course, she came home with us!

We didn't have Rascal too long, and to be honest, I don't quite remember why, but I do remember that we found her a good home with a single lady who worked with Larry's mother. The last we heard, Rascal was the center of attention at her house, with no other pets or children for competition. She even slept in her mistress' bed.

21. THE INEVITABLE DECISION

Through all this, we still had our faithful Schnitzel! He was showing the usual signs of age. His eyes were glazed with cataracts and we caught him walking in front of oncoming cars. When he stopped obeying us, we realized he couldn't hear our commands. Worst of all, he had developed prostrate trouble, like an old man. He was having accidents everywhere, especially in the laundry closet. Larry pointed out that if one of the human family members was causing all this extra work, I wouldn't put up with it. So, we made the agonizing decision that his "quality of life" had declined to such depths that the only humane thing to do was to have him put down.

I honestly don't remember the fateful day. I don't remember telling the children or taking him to the vet or saying goodbye. I think the mind sometimes erases the sad times in life. What I do remember is that for 16 years, he was loyal and always tried to please us. He was gentle with the children and brought us all a lot of laughs. I don't know if it's because he was our first real pet or if he really was that smart, or if it's that we raised him with our children, but 30 years later, he stands out in my mind as the most special of all our animals.

22. BETWEEN THE SCHNITZELS

Scouting has been an important tradition in the Myers family, so it was no surprise that our son advanced rapidly to the rank of Eagle Scout. To receive this award, he had to complete an approved service project. He chose to do some painting and repair at the Girl Scout camp, and upon arrival, he found that the ranger's German shorthair pointer had just delivered a litter of pups that looked very much like the neighbor's labrador retriever.

Of course they all needed homes, so not only did Eric agree to take one, but he convinced Larry's brother to take one of the others. Uncle Bill always named his dogs after friends, so this one was "Bob" and he soon outweighed his litter mate by 20 pounds. Eric was concerned and quizzed his uncle about the dog's diet. The answer was

"French fries, hamburgers or whatever I'm eating!" As for me, I was very glad that we had lucked out and gotten the smaller dog. His name was "Charcoal"; you can guess what color he was! He turned out to be a wonderful pet.

"Charky," the diminutive given him by nine year-old Mindy, lived for weekend trips to the lake. The retriever half of him loved to swim, so when his human family went for a dip in the lake, he would join us, noisily dog-paddling around. He alternated between climbing onto my lap while I was settled in my floating chair or crawling onto Mindy's air mattress with her. This always caused shrieks from her and cries of "Charky's going to sink me!"

When we went out in the boat to go fishing, he would dive into the water and chase us. While the boat's motor was only a 35 hp. outboard, his fastest dog paddle was no match for it. He was nearly as determined as our Schnitzel had been, and would not give up. About 200 yards out into the lake, Mindy would tearfully beg her father to stop and rescue him. Larry usually relented and we would pull the dog into the already crowded boat. Everyone knows what dogs do when they're wet; they shake water everywhere, plus Charky would show his gratitude for being allowed aboard by leaping around giving each of us a very wet kiss. All the while, the boat is rocking, Mindy is still sniffling, Eric is laughing and their father is yelling!

While it's true that Charcoal loved to go to the lake, it was sometimes a challenge to get him there, because he tended to get carsick. There was one ten-mile section of road that was very curvy and hilly; this is where the problem usually occurred.

One weekend, Larry and the children had gone on ahead and Charcoal was riding with me in the front seat of my company car. On the third steep hill, I heard a groan and then a loud roar and Charcoal leaned over on me. When I realized he was going to be sick, I turned his head so it was directly over the waste basket between my bucket seats. At the same time, I'm steering the car and trying desperately to find a place to pull off the two-lane road.

I'm not sure what he had eaten, but the smell was enough to bring tears to my eyes! Without soap and water, I simply threw the whole wastebasket into a ditch. After a short walk and rest, we climbed back into the car and drove as slowly as possible to our destination. Despite vacuuming and deodorizer and fresh air, the car smelled for two weeks!

23. THE FORTY POUND BLACK "FISH"

.One hot July day, Larry and I were relaxing in the air-conditioned mobile home and the kids and Charcoal were down at the dock, fishing. Suddenly, Mindy came flying in the door, out of breath from running the quarter mile from the lake. Wide-eyed and sobbing, she said, "Charky ate a fish hook!" Surely she was exaggerating; the dog wasn't dumb enough to eat a hook.

We all rushed to the car, and when we came upon the scene, here was our son, holding the dog, and sticking out of its mouth was a fishing line, still attached to a rod and reel. One of the kids had laid it down on the dock, and apparently the bait looked like an appetizer to a hungry dog.

We loaded children, dog-- fishing rod and all-- into the car and raced 20 miles to the nearest vet, who clipped the line off in his mouth and said, "Hopefully, he'll pass the hook." (Our own vet later told us this was the wrong thing to do; it would have been better if he'd had more line to work with.)

We took him back to the trailer and he seemed to be feeling surprisingly well, walking around and wagging his tail, until he took a drink of water and tried to swallow. Then he yelped in pain and jumped into my lap, as if to say, "Help, Mom!" At that point, we packed up and headed home to our own vet, arriving just before closing time on Saturday afternoon.

After X-rays, he determined it was a treble hook (three prongs) and was lodged right next to the heart. There was not much possibility that he would pass it. The only chance was to do surgery, using a new instrument that he had never tried. It had a mirror so he could insert it down the dog's throat and try to wiggle the hook loose. Now the decision: Did we want to spend half-month's salary on a mutt? We looked at each other, then looked at our children's worried faces and then remembered the dog's anguished cries when he tried to swallow. Of course, the answer was yes.

The doctor was able to remove the hook and asked if he could keep it to show at a veterinary meeting, because it was so amazing that his new instrument was able to retrieve it. We went home to anxiously wait, while Charcoal stayed in the hospital soaking up antibiotics and running up his bill. He survived and lived to run and swim another day!

24. BARON VON SCHNITZEL II

Charky was a gentle, affectionate pet, but we all missed our funny little wiener dog, so after two dachshundless years, we bought another puppy. Since he looked exactly like Schnitz, that's what we named him. The thinking was that we would probably all call him that anyway, so we might as well make that his registered name.

Shortly after we got him, we realized it was not going to work to have a large mixed lab in the house with a five-pound puppy. Charcoal was a little too inquisitive about the new dog's sex, and would not leave him alone. We discussed getting a dog house for Charky, but since he had been raised as an indoor dog and was accustomed to sleeping in Eric's bed, we all agreed he would not be happy living in the back yard. I couldn't bear to take him to a shelter, so we started looking for a good home for him.

The secretary at my office lived on a farm outside the city and had lots of room for him to run and a pond for him to swim, plus she had two little girls to play with him, so when she agreed to take him, it seemed like a good fit. We bade him a tearful farewell and I bundled all his toys and his blankie and took him to the office. When she later told me that he was the "weirdest dog" because he sat at the front gate all day watching the road, it broke my heart. I knew he was waiting for us to come back, which of course we never did! It's the one pet decision I regretted. I felt we abandoned him in favor of a thoroughbred. Even though he was a "mutt," he was an obedient friend and deserved better from us.

25. THE FISH POND PROJECT

No narrative aboutMyers pets would be complete without mentioning fish. Larry and Eric are both avid fishermen (another family tradition). The first fish pond was built while Larry was recuperating from open heart surgery. Back then (1980), this was a relatively new procedure and he was told to stay quiet for 4 weeks after his hospital stay. Desperately needing a project, he decided to install an in-ground fish pond in the backyard. The only problem was he wasn't physically able to do the work, so he enlisted the children and me to do the digging. I can still see him sitting in a lawn chair supervising! After many hours of work, we were ready to pour the concrete. A cement mixer backed into the back yard and dumped its load into the excavation and we quickly smoothed it out. The next step was to apply a sealant to make sure the water didn't leak out. This had to set for 48 hours, and then we filled it with water from the garden hose, which took several hours. Then it had to set overnight to be chlorine-free before we could add the fish.

The big day arrived. I rushed downstairs and looked out the window and was astounded to see the pond was empty! Either an elephant had sneaked in for a drink, or all the water had leaked out overnight! Needless to say, Larry was not too happy! But not to be deterred, he went to a farm supply store and bought a three by six-foot cattle tank to put down into the concrete pond. When it was delivered, one of the neighbors thought it was for some sort of hydrotherapy for Larry!

The next task he devised for us was to take my company van out to a rock quarry and haul back large rocks to put around the edge. There was still a gap since the concrete pond had been poured in a free-form design. This was filled with dirt which we had to haul and shovel in. Then, flowers were planted so that it looked like a planned landscape. Actually, it looked surprisingly nice! Rather than having tropical fish in his "pond," Larry wanted to be different and decided to stock it with game fish. Any time he caught a small bass or crappie, he carefully transported it home and put it in the tank.

The fish pond flourished for eight years until we moved. The new owner's toddler fell in the first week, and so they filled in the tank and did away with Larry's carefully planned "pond."

26. THE LITTLE BROWN GROUCH

We soon learned that dogs, even among the same breed, have distinctive personalities just like people, and the second Schnitz was not as easy going as his predecessor. In later years, we referred to him as "the grumpy Schnitz" because he was easily irritated and growled a lot. Of course, this was the pet of Mindy's high school years and he spent a lot of time in her room. While researching this book, I learned that she and her friend Lisa, used to dress him up and play "dolls" with him. This may well have contributed to his disgruntled disposition.

Mindy's room was a mix of femininity and teenage grunge. She had a fluffy dust ruffle that came to the floor around her canopy bed. This masked anything she chose to hide underneath. What we didn't realize was that

Schnitz was using it as his personal toilette, and when we moved, we discovered a yellow stain outlining the bed. He definitely had marked his territory! Oops!

Both of our children were very creative when it came to nicknames. Schnitzel became Schnitz, then Snitzy, then "Itsy", then Itzy-Bon, then Bon Bon Bean and ultimately, just "Bean". For some reason, Bean is the moniker that stuck, so Mindy and her friends all called the dog, "Bean" and he responded to it. (Years later, when Mindy was living on her own, she bought her first pet, a dachshund and his registered name was "Bean". He was followed by a younger "brother," Ham.)

After meeting my boss' poodle and seeing his repertoire of tricks, Mindy was determined to teach Schnitz to roll over on command. I think her exact words were, "Bean's as smart as that little yappy poodle!" And he was! In short order, she taught him to roll over, first with a voice command and then, with just a hand signal. Sometimes he would roll all across the room, hoping for a reward treat, which he always got, of course!

Another talent was his extraordinary jumping ability. Our yard had large trees and an equally large squirrel population, and he was determined to catch one! He would jump five feet up the tree chasing the bushy tailed rodents, then fall to the ground and bark incessantly. He could be two flights up in our split-level home and in a normal voice, we'd say "squirrel!"

Bean would come flying down the stairs, his feet touching about every third step, brown ears extended like rudders, all the while whining in a high-pitched cry. We'd pretend to have trouble getting the door open and that only added to his excitement. When we finally let him out, he'd head for the tree, the squirrel just ahead of him. In six years, he never came close to catching one, but he never gave up! There's that dachshund determination we so admired in the first place!

27. A CANINE ROMANCE

My college friend, Jennifer, moved to Overland Park in the mid-eighties with her daughters and an adorable little female dachshund named "Uta." Uta was a miniature, like Schnitz, but she had a much smaller frame. Not having the advantage of a fenced yard in which to exercise and unlimited squirrels to chase, Uta had packed on a few extra pounds. Actually, she outweighed our long, lean Schnitz by about 30 percent! On her visits, she tried so hard to keep up with him, panting with the effort and pumping with her short little legs.

We noticed that Schnitz was not his usual grumpy self around Uta; rather, he mellowed out as if he was trying to be on his best behavior around her. One weekend, Jennifer had an out-of-town meeting and needed a pet sitter, so Uta came for a sleepover! Schnitz was very excited to see her, and when she arrived, he ran in circles, barked and even did his rollover trick to impress her. Uta brought her blankie, but as I recall, they both slept curled together in the middle of Mindy's bed!

28. ANOTHER HARD DECISION

After both children left for college, things were much quieter in our home, and soon we noticed that Schnitz was sleeping a lot, or at least staying in one location. He had difficulty in climbing the stair in our tri-level house. His condition worsened, and the vet diagnosed him as having the back problem that is so common to his breed. He suggested that we confine him, and absolutely no jumping! Remember, this is the Schnitz who would leap five feet up the tree to chase a squirrel! In retrospect, this talent, combined with his rollover trick, may have contributed to his back problem!

Larry and I had a trip planned to Las Vegas, so we decided to board the dog and let the doctor treat him while we were gone. Confining him to a kennel would prevent further damage to his spine. About three days into our vacation, we received a phone call from the sympathetic vet, telling us that "this little guy is just not responding to treatment." He didn't want us to come home, expecting him to be healed.

Our choices were (1) a very expensive surgery which might help temporarily but was no guarantee that the condition wouldn't reoccur, or (2) euthanasia. I remember lots of crying (on my part) and hugging and discussing, until we reached the painful decision. With two children in college, we simply could not afford a big canine medical bill.

Larry called the doctor back and told him to put him to sleep before we returned home. It was too painful to see him again. He was only six years old, and based on our experience with Schnitzel I, who lived to be 15, we had assumed he had many years left! We didn't tell Mindy until she came home for Thanksgiving vacation, and I remember the tearful scene. She was very upset that we didn't tell her when it happened.

After this traumatic event, it was my decision that we should NOT get another dog. I simply could not face this again. Anyone who has loved an animal and then loses it should understand. They become such an integral part of the family, yet they are with us such a short time! I discussed this with my husband and assumed that he was in total agreement! At this point, we had been married 27 years, and I should have learned to never assume! Apparently, he thought I meant we shouldn't get another dachshund because of their genetic health problems!

29. THE POSTER PUPPY

It was only after I started this book that I learned he got the idea for our next pet from a poster that hung on our daughter's bedroom wall. It pictured an adorable puppy reclining in a hammock. Shortly after Schnitz died, he questioned Mindy as to the breed of the dog in the picture. Upon learning it was a beagle, he did some research and decided that beagles were a very healthy breed and normally had no congenital defects. He located a breeder outside the city, and while I was working one afternoon, he visited her and picked out a two month-old female beagle puppy!

Larry had a very tender heart, but he didn't always think things through before acting on them! All he knew is that I was sad and missing Schnitz, and he thought a cute little puppy (and she was) would cheer me up. What he didn't consider is that we had our house on the market and it had to be kept neat at all times. New puppies are seldom neat. Also, it was November, and with the busiest and coldest time of the year coming up, it was not the best time for potty training.

Nevertheless, she was ours – bought, paid for and registered with the AKC. We named her for our two mothers, "Beulah Lucille," and called her Lucy. We quickly learned that Lucy had a mind of her own and was as determined as our dachshunds had been; the difference was, she didn't seem to be as smart! The season of the year didn't matter; Lucy showed no interest in housebreaking in any season! We were advised to buy her a kennel because "dogs will never soil the place where they sleep!" Wrong! After scrubbing and disinfecting the kennel the tenth time, we decided to strategically place newspapers and make the whole kitchen her kennel. We used 12-inch table leaves to blockade the doors. She knocked one down and it frightened her so much that even as a

full grown adult dog, she never figured out that she could jump over (almost step over) and escape. If prospective buyers were coming, we had to quickly gather the papers, mop the kitchen floor and throw Lucy into the kennel. From there she would look mournfully through the screen and draw comments about the "darling" puppy.

MO sitting on our white plastic couch.
Norfolk, VA. 1960

The first Schnitzel in his beer box by our bed…1963

The children with Chester,
the hunting dog who never hunted…circa 1971

Beulah Lucille, LUCY, the errant beagle, 1988

Schnitz meets his first cat, baby Pouncer. 1991

Pouncer in his Christmas bow,
ready for the holidays, 2000

Roy keeps a watchful eye on his charge, 2002

Schnitzel III in his winter snowman scarf, 1999

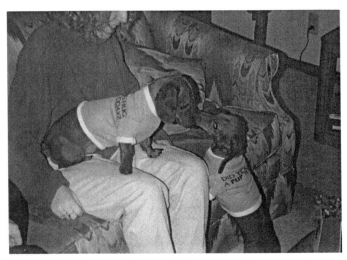

Schnitz and Bean show off their new Christmas shirts, which ask the question Did You Hug a Pup Today

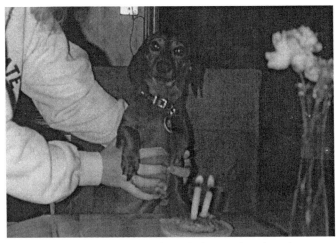

Schnitz celebates his 2nd birthday with a hamburger cake, 1991

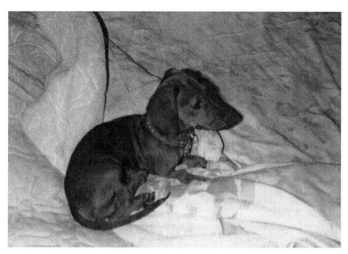

Schnitzel's favorite place to spend a winter afternoon…
in his master's bed!

Cuddles watches the pool robot. Florida, 2007

30. LUCY'S NEW "DIGS"

Eventually, the house sold, and when Lucy was about six months old, we moved to a larger and newer home. This one had even more woodwork for Lucy to chew on and more carpet for her to soil. Thus she ended up in the kitchen again, with the same table leaves blocking the doorways. We tried confining her to a basement laundry room, and twenty years later, the wood door still bears her teeth marks. The first thing we had to do after moving in was spend an additional $3,000 for a fence to keep Lucy in the backyard.

During the three-week time span between moving day and waiting for the fence installation, I would attempt to walk my cute new puppy. It actually was a series of jerks and stops and lunges; in no sense of the imagination could it be called a walk! My only respite was when we would meet children along the route. They would pet her and comment on her "cuteness" and Lucy would stand quietly and wag her tail. If she broke loose from me (a frequent occurrence), I looked for anyone under four feet tall and yelled at them to catch her.

At last the fence was installed and we thought it would solve all our problems. Lucy would have a large area to run and play and chase rabbits, yet she'd be confined and safe. Hopefully, she would do all her toilet duties outside, also! Imagine my surprise when I let her out by herself the first time, and within five minutes, I heard this very loud, mournful wail. Of course I knew beagles were hounds and hounds howl, but how could such a loud noise come from a ten-pound puppy, and more importantly, WHY was she howling?

When I went to investigate, she was gone from the secure backyard with the $3,000 fence! It seems that where our fence joined the neighbor's fence, a small "alley was created, approximately five inches wide. Lucy had sniffed her way into the space and wasn't smart enough to figure out that she could turn around, or back out the same way she entered. Instead, she simply threw her head back and howled! Of course, it was too small for me to squeeze in after her. The only solution I could come up with was to grab a hot dog, walk through two yards to the other end of the tunnel and holding the treat for her to see, coax her out. Then I could scoop her up and carry her home. Thus began a tradition of using the hot dog treat to lure her back from one of her misadventures!

We had lived in the neighborhood only two months when Lucy escaped one hot summer evening. We were dressed to go out to dinner, but I took out running in my high heels, hot dog in hand, to retrieve her. She led me across the street, through neighbors' yards to the next block, with me running behind her, waving at people I hadn't even met. We ran through a sprinkler and finally, she spotted some children playing on their swing set. "Grab her!" I yelled.

After carrying her home and giving her the hot dog, I had to shower and change clothes, and of course, we were late for the dinner engagement. There's something wrong with this picture: Why am I rewarding this kind of behavior with a treat? Maybe she wasn't so dumb!

Another chase adventure occurred one Saturday morning. I had scheduled an open house for my Tupperware customers. Fortunately I had one of my trainees to help, because a neighbor child knocked on the door, and with an innocent lisp informed me, "Woocie's in our yard." I left hasty instructions with my assistant, grabbed a hot dog and took out running. I would get within six feet of the dog, thrust the treat in front of me and calmly call her. Just when I was ready to reach for her, she'd take off. It became a great game for her and the scene was repeated several times until we were about a half-mile from home and nearing a major highway. Finally, this 50-year-old, slightly out of shape woman decided she didn't really care what happened to this unruly canine. I turned and at a more leisurely pace, walked home.

By the time I got there, the guilt had settled in, so I got the car and drove around the neighborhood looking for her. Anyone I saw, I stopped and gave them a business card and asked them to call if they saw a small tri-colored beagle.

When I got home, I went into the kitchen for a drink of water, and sitting innocently on the back porch was Lucy! To this day, I don't know if she had beaten me home or if I had been following a different dog. I strongly suspect it was another beagle who was running for her life to escape this crazed woman chasing her with a hot dog!

The kicker to this story came the next day when the phone rang and a man said, "I have your beagle in my garage." I said, "No, I think my beagle is here, but better let me check." She was.

31. LUCY GOES TO SCHOOL

The months went by and this pattern of behavior continued. Lucy lived in the kitchen with her 12-inch barriers, and the family and any visitors had to step over them. She had daily accidents in the kitchen, in spite of the fact that we let her outside at regular intervals. Often she would clean up her mess by eating it! We had never had a pet like this. Larry always prided himself on being a good animal trainer, but Lucy seemed to be beyond training, plus she acted as if she just didn't like us!

Finally we decided to seek professional help. Upon checking, the only dog training class I could find was offered on Thursday evenings. If I took her (and I was the logical choice since I was at home with her more), I would have to give up six Thursday evenings. Since Thursday was the most popular night for my Tupperware parties, this would be very costly. Each lesson would cost about $150.

When I pointed this out to my spouse, his response was," Well, I'm not taking her!" (It might have meant missing a favorite TV show or a Royals game.) So the idea of Lucy's classes died, or at least was tabled.

Several weeks later, I returned home from a Tupperware party about 9:30 p.m. to find Larry and Lucy running around the living room. The dog had the remote control in her mouth and her master was slowly circling, then lunging and she would run away. Lucy seemed to be thoroughly enjoying this new game. When I entered the scene, Larry threw up his hands and yelled, "I GIVE UP! ENROLL US!"

Lucy was the center of attention in her class. Everyone commented on her "cuteness," and since she was the smallest dog of ten, she was a little intimidated by the German shepherds and golden retrievers. She actually did very well, and graduated with honors. She had learned to sit, stay and heel. The only problem is she still wouldn't come when you called her.

The instructor had a solution for one problem. Lucy's main source of entertainment when we let her out to exercise was digging! We soon gave up worrying about the holes in the yard, although it was a little hazardous when mowing. Sometimes the wheel would drop into one of Lucy's holes. Larry decided to limit any landscaping efforts to the front yard, since the back was hopeless as long as we owned this small tri-colored digging machine.

He accepted this, but it was another matter when the TV kept going out and we discovered the source of the problem. In our neighborhood, the cable is required to be buried and Lucy was digging it up! The dog trainer suggested that we set mouse traps everywhere she had dug. The theory was that if she tried to dig, she would trip the trap and it would frighten her so that she would not do it again. This could work! After all, this is the dog that was afraid of her 12-inch table leaf!

Larry invested in a supply of mouse traps, spent two hours setting them all and positioning them in her favorite digging spots. Then we let her out for a test run. She made a beeline for the closest trap, set it off and jumped back in surprise. She raised her head, let out her characteristic howl, and then proceeded to continue digging! Then, she chewed up the mouse trap!

After another few months, we had to admit that the dog obedience classes had not helped. This pet was no fun! She only created extra work for us both, and brought no pleasure! Perhaps she'd be happier on a farm or at least in the country. Remembering how upset our daughter had been when we put the last Schnitz down without telling her, I called her at college to tell her we were giving up on Lucy. Her only comment was, "You're the ones who have to live with her!"

We ran an ad in the Kansas City Star on a cold Sunday morning. We had at least a dozen calls before 9 a.m. from people wanting a registered beagle. One was a single mother whose little boy wanted a "Snoopy dog." However, they had no fence and were planning to confine her in the garage. Larry and I looked at each other and said, "That little boy thinks he can play with her," and we both knew she'd run away. Fortunately, a man arrived first and bought her to hunt rabbits. He had other beagles and was familiar with the breed. We warned him that Lucy didn't mind too well (or at all), but he laughed it off and insisted that she would just follow the older dogs.

About two weeks later, we had a phone call from a woman saying, "I have your dog." Seems Lucy was still wearing her tags with our contact info. I knew there was a reason to keep the new owner's phone number! When I called, his wife answered and said he was out with the dogs. "That must be why he's late – he's probably looking for Lucy. You know, she just won't come when you call her!" REALLY! That was the last we heard of Beulah Lucille.

32. BIFF THE PREPPY GERBIL

Over the years, there was more than one rodent pet, but one stands out in my mind. Mindy was in her freshman year at K-State and her big brother wanted to get her a memorable Christmas gift. After a trip to the local pet store, he decided on a cute little brown gerbil (Is there any other color?) Of course, if he was going to live in a girls' dorm, he needed his own quarters, so Eric also bought a plastic cage called a "Habitrail" and a rolling plastic ball for his workouts. Mindy was thrilled with her present and christened him "Biff the Preppy Gerbil."

The first problem surfaced when her transportation back to college objected to having that "rat" in his car. He finally relented when assured that Biff would be secure in his cage.

The second problem arose when it became apparent that gerbils are nocturnal and humans are not. When the lights went out, Biff was ready to run nosily on his exercise wheel in the Habitrail, and Mindy's roommate was not too happy. They solved this by removing the wheel from the cage and making sure to put Biff in his portable exercise ball every evening. The theory was that he would tire himself out and maybe sleep during the night. The girls learned to close their doors or he would "roll in" for a visit and sometimes got himself stuck behind a bed or desk.

Biff made it through the semester and then came home for the summer. I remember he spent every night in the upstairs hallway because he was still very noisy! In the fall, the happy "couple" headed back to school, this time to take up residence in the sorority house. This lasted one semester, until executive council outlawed all rodents in residence! The rumor was that Biff got loose and frightened some of the sisters! Seems not everyone thinks gerbils are "cute."

33. THE OFFICE GERBIL

Thus it was that Biff ended up residing in my lower level office in our home. I think Mindy's rationale for that was "I'm putting him there so you won't forget to feed him. If he's upstairs in my bedroom, you'll never see him." (This had some appeal to me-- if he was in the basement office, he wouldn't disturb us). Every morning, after checking e-mail, I checked Biff's food and water and even talked to him. This is proof that mothers will do almost anything for their children!

Everything went well for several months. Biff appeared to be healthy and relatively happy, probably because he could run and play at will all night long. Finally, the day arrived for his "mommy" to return home for summer vacation. When I walked in from my Tupperware party that evening, she met me at the door with a tearful, query, "MOM…where is Biff?"

Seems he had nosed open the top to his cage and escaped! I assured her that he couldn't have gone far, and with both of us looking, we could find him. He had to be in the finished basement somewhere! (Didn't he?) After moving all the furniture in my office, we started on the family room. We checked behind the piano and couches. Finally, bleary-eyed, I convinced Mindy that we should go to bed and continue the search the next morning. I promised to make it my first priority since it was "my fault."

This is the night I learned a useful fact that I will probably never need to recall unless Jeff Foxworthy calls me to be on "Are You Smarter Than a Fifth Grader?" *Gerbils can climb!* About 3 a.m., my spouse woke me from a dead sleep with an ominous warning: "There's something in this bed!" He went on to say that he wasn't implying it was the missing rodent, but *something!* I turned on the light, and there between my legs, on top of the covers, was

Biff, sitting on his haunches and looking at me. Unbelievable as it seems, he had climbed 20 steps from the basement, made his way down the hall and into the master bedroom and then

onto the bed! "Grab him!" I screamed. "I'm not touching that thing!" Seems Larry didn't think he was too cute, either. I guess, as they say, beauty IS in the eye of the beholder!

Showing remarkable agility for my age, I sat up and caught him, returning him promptly to his cage and securing the cover with several heavy books. Not long after that, Biff went the way of the other hamsters and gerbils we had owned, and died a natural death.

Twenty years later, Biff's "mommy" still thought little rodents were cute, and assured by the pet store that they only sold males, allowed her children to get two teddy bear hamsters. Imagine her surprise when, two weeks later, she came home to find six babies! To add to the nightmare, the adults were using them as a late night snack. She quickly went and bought two more cages, one for the babies and one for the mother. Who could determine the sex of a hamster? The only solution was to separate them.

The store offered to take the babies, but when Mindy heard they often use them as snake food, she couldn't bear to return them. With the hamster population growing at an alarming rate, she advertised them "free to good homes" on Craig's List and permanently closed the hamster breeding operation. Lesson learned!

34. THE LAST OF THE SCHNITZELS

Larry and I were empty nesters for only a few months after Lucy was gone when it was time for Mindy to return home for the summer. It was a beautiful Sunday afternoon and just happened to be Mother's Day. I'm not sure which of us came up with the idea to check the classified section for "Livestock for Sale", but in quick order we were in the car headed to a Missouri suburb to just "look" at a litter of miniature dachshunds. This wasn't a breeder, just a family who had bred their pet.

The puppies were romping around the yard, falling over each other and looking adorable as only puppies can. The family had even named them, and we fell in love with the runt of the litter, whom they called "Brutus." He wasn't the most handsome; in fact, he was a little peculiar looking. His coat was fuzzy, and while he was the reddish-brown color of our Schnitzels, he had a black stripe down the center of his back! What he lacked in size and appearance, he made up in spirit and personality, and of course, he went home with us

They had called him Brutus because he was such a tough little guy, but in the Myers home, he became Baron von Schnitzel III! What else?

He inherited Lucy's basket, equipped with a blue velour pillow, a hand-knit afghan and an old leopard-print blanket. He settled in quickly to the household routine and soon learned that he was to "do his business" outside. I think he remembered playing in the grass with his litter mates, because he was always excited to go out. Or course, it was summer in Kansas and like his predecessors, he was very cold natured and preferred the heat to air-conditioning.

By the time he was six months old, Schnitz' coat had smoothed out and was no longer fuzzy, and his coloring had evened out. It was only when he was agitated or upset at something (like another animal, for instance) that you could see the dark stripe down his back.

35. "ROTOROOTER DOG"

Schnitz soon learned that his covers were much warmer if they were on *top* of his body. If no human was around to tuck him in, he would stick his long nose under the edge of the blanket, throw his head back and then twist his body, turning in a circle until he was completely covered. Only then would he lie down and go to sleep. To the uninformed, it just looked like a small lump in the basket. He repeated this routine any time he was instructed to "get in your box" or if he had simply had enough of h u m a n conversation

and was ready to retire for the night. This was a constant source of amusement for our guests.

Of all the dogs, this one fit the description of "lap dog" most aptly. It could be that, with the children grown and moved to their own greener pastures, there was usually a lap more readily available. The minute I would sit down on the couch to read or watch television, he would jump up and arrange his ten-pound body over my legs. We called him, "the drape."

In lieu of a child to bond with, he attached himself to me and was my constant shadow. If I went to my lower-level office and forgot him, I would soon hear a high-pitched whine outside the door. He would lie on the floor next to my desk, and in the winter, he would find a place by the space heater, edging so close that his fur would feel hot to the touch. I worried that he might spontaneously combust.

36. POUNCER RUGLEY

Schnitzel III was only two years old when his status was challenged and his tranquility disturbed by a new pet, this one of the feline species! I need to preface this chapter by saying that Larry Myers had absolutely NO regard for cats of any kind! In fact, I had often heard him say, "The only good cat is a dead cat!" Of course, he had never been around a cat let alone owned one. He had instilled this prejudice in his son also. However, Eric had a girlfriend who loved cats, and he had already experienced a change of heart.

The family was gathered in Manhattan, Kan. for Mindy's college graduation. It was a proud and happy occasion, until her roommate unveiled her gift: a very small gold kitten that her vet-student boyfriend had rescued from a barn. He was just the color of the carpet in the girls' apartment, so they named him "Rugley."

Everyone gathered around, making appropriate remarks and commenting on his cute factor, except Larry, who roared, "OH, NO! NOT IN MY HOUSE!"

We spent an hour lobbying for the cat. Nearly everyone else had had experience with felines, and we extolled their many virtues. Finally, Larry agreed to give him a chance, just until Mindy could find a job and move into her own place. There were two stipulations: first, he would not be allowed out of Mindy's room and second, if he had even one accident outside the litter box, he was GONE! Larry couldn't believe that any animal would actually climb into a toidy box!

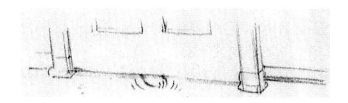

So it was that after 31 years of marriage, a cat came into our home for the first time. He was very playful (as all kittens are) and could jump ten times his height, which was about six inches, so Mindy called him "Pouncer" and relegated Rugley to a middle name. The living arrangement actually worked out well. I remember walking by the closed door and seeing a little paw protruding under it.

Mindy spent a lot of time in her room, playing with him and talking to him. I always felt this helped socialize him, and in later years, he never ran and hid as so many cats do; rather, he wanted to be the center of attention (and usually was!)

Schnitz adjusted surprisingly well to having a cat in the house. Of course, they didn't meet face to face very often. The dog would position himself outside the bedroom door, long nose to the carpet, trying to nip at the small gold paw that would shoot out. There was no need to push a friendship, because Pouncer would be moving out soon. This happened within three months, and after a few paychecks, Mindy was ready to venture out on her own. Around Thanksgiving, she and Pouncer moved to their new quarters, sharing an apartment with two other young women. Larry and I settled back to our one pet household.

Less than a week passed and I had a tearful phone call from Mindy. Seems one of the roommates was allergic to our sweet kitten and "I have to find a home for Pouncer. He says he'd much prefer to live with "Grandma and Grandpa", so "would you please talk to Dad?" Who would have thought our first grandchild would have four legs!

After softening him up with his favorite dinner, I broached the subject to Larry. His initial reaction was just what I expected – an emphatic NO! (Do I know this man after thirty plus years of marriage?) But after an hour of pointing out how sweet and cute and clean this little animal was, he relented and agreed to give him a chance. So it was that Pouncer came back to live with us.

Then the most amazing thing happened! After a few months, Larry could see that all the cat virtues I had pointed out were absolutely true, and he and Pouncer bonded! Not only was he allowed out of the bedroom, he had full run of the house and it soon became apparent that he was to be "Grandpa's kitty"!

37. GRANDPA'S KITTY

Pouncer grew into a very handsome cat, soon outweighing his canine counterpart. This Schnitz was much easier to get along with than the grumpy Schnitzel II, so the two animals co-mingled peacefully, sometimes even sharing food and water. The cat had one idiosyncrasy. He preferred running water to drink; so when he heard the sink or the bathtub, he would come flying, jump up and contort his body to drink from the faucet. Even an accidental plunge in the tub didn't deter him! When we went out of town, Larry insisted on leaving the bathtub dripping slightly, because Pouncer liked it!

If there was any problem, it was that he was too quiet! Neither of us was used to an animal that would stealthily creep into the room, as if he were stalking and startle not only the dog but any humans who happened to be there. This problem was solved by investing in a cat collar, complete with a bell and his registration tags. This way, we could always know where he was, and he didn't seem to object to the neckwear.

He was definitely a "people" cat and always wanted to be near his humans and their guests. It was a Sunday afternoon ritual to have our mothers (the "Grannies") over to play cards. We would pull the kitchen desk chair over and Pouncer would curl up on the seat, frequently stretching and nudging the closest hand for a pat on the head. He especially pestered Larry's mom, who, like her son, had never been fond of cats. He won her over completely by demanding her attention any time she was in the house.

Pouncer was strictly an indoor cat and was almost never allowed outside; until Larry decided he needed some fresh air. After some research, he purchased a cat harness and leash. The problem was that Pouncer had never stepped on grass (at least not since he was a tiny kitten on the farm and apparently he didn't remember that)! Totally baffled by the different texture, he would lift each foot up to his shoulder and lean at a 90 degree angle. We joked that Larry was taking him for a "drag." Although Larry persisted, it was not meant to be. You could safely say the cat won this one!

38. THE VISITING FELINES

Everything was tranquil in our empty nest, until Eric called from Colorado, telling us he wanted to move back to Kansas. Could he stay with us until he found a job and could get his own place? Of course, we would never deny our firstborn a roof over his head even when he told us he was bringing his two large tomcats with him! After all, it was just a temporary arrangement!

Driving 700 miles alone with the two cats, Eric had to stop after dark to allow the cats to relieve themselves. Rufus, a 20-pound black Maine coon cat, wandered off and it was impossible to see him in the dark. Even though he was a very savvy cat, he didn't respond when called. Eric spent several anxious moments looking for him;

thank goodness for his glowing golden eyes. They finally arrived home, tired but safe.

Now the problem was, where should we put the cats? Pouncer, as the resident cat, obviously had priority, but the visitors both outweighed him by at least six pounds. Eric always chooses the largest male cats he can find to rescue from a shelter, so both Rufus and his white counterpart, Goober, were 20-plus pounds. We all agreed that we should keep the cats separated to prevent trouble, so it was decided to confine the visitors in a basement storage room during the day. At night, Pouncer could sleep in the bedroom with his masters and the big cats could roam. We forgot to take into account that Rufus still had all his claws, which he used to systematically shred the basement bathroom carpet.

After a month or so, we decided to introduce the "boys." After a period of pacing and circling and sniffing, they seemed to accept the situation. Actually, they didn't have much choice! Poor Schnitz hid in his bed, certain that the cats were taking over his house.

One afternoon, Eric ran down the stairs to my office with the ominous query, "Where are the cats?" He could hear the unmistakable sounds of a big time cat fight! When we found them, two flights up in a bedroom, Pouncer and Goober were clawing and wrestling and Rufus was growling at them both, as if he was trying to mediate. From all the gold fur on the carpet, it looked as if Pouncer was getting the worst of it. Back to "Plan A" or "operation separation!"

Fortunately, Eric found a job and his own apartment in about six months. I think the landlord knew he had *one* cat, but he managed to keep the second one a secret. Both Rufus and Goober were part of the package when Eric and Katy married, and both cats lived into their late teens becoming part of his family.

39. A NEW GRANDDOG!

Eric and his bride agreed to wait until they had a house and a yard to buy a dog, so as soon as the closing date was set on their two-story house in the neighborhood where Eric grew up, they starting looking at different breeds. With characteristic eagerness, Eric surprised her with a golden retriever puppy and brought him home on "moving day." Like his father, he rarely stopped to consider consequences! In his defense, he had never been directly involved in moving an entire household! Guess who got to babysit the newest little Myers while they were settling in?

This cute little guy was christened Roy Williams Myers, in honor of the Kansas basketball coach. Several years later, when the human Roy defected to North

Carolina, there was talk of changing the dog's name to Roy "Clark" Myers but cooler heads prevailed and his registered moniker remained the same. Roy was about 10 pounds at two months, the size of our adult dachshund and had very large paws. (This should have been a clue).

He grew, almost overnight, into a 125-lb. rambunctious tornado, charging into the house, clearing the coffee table with his tail and greeting any one in sight with wet, sloppy kisses!

If you went to his house, he would greet you enthusiastically at the door with his trademark welcoming bark and kiss. Visitors soon learned to hold out a foot to fend him off, or brace their bodies in case he decided to put his paws on their shoulders. To this day, Roy is strictly an "indoor" dog. When he is ready to re-enter the house after his bathroom break, he simply looks in the family room window and barks. He sleeps in the king-sized bed with his masters, serving as an extra blanket in the wintertime.

He allows his "feline brothers" to groom him by licking his long blond fur and amazingly, he is intimidated by the largest (22-lb.) cat, Zeus. If Roy happens to be sitting in the recliner (which he often is) and Zeus enters, he relinquishes his seat to the cat.

When the children arrived he served as a big pillow or a pony for them to ride on. Anything the toddlers could dish out, Roy would take, never becoming cross or nipping at them, although certainly they deserved it at times. Good dogs seem to instinctively know that little children don't know any better. He doesn't get a lot of exercise, being confined to a kennel while his humans are at work. I'm sure this has contributed to his large girth.

When Eric and Katy took the children to Disneyland a few years ago, Aunt Mindy was kind enough to take Roy for the two weeks they were gone. The only problem is, Mindy's very cold-blooded and keeps the heat in her townhome cranked up. Poor Roy was used to much cooler temperatures and his lush fur coat added to the problem. He panted non-stop and drooled on furniture, rugs and clothing indiscriminately! I'm sure the dog thought he'd been abandoned by his family and banished to some sort of hell. Everyone was glad when they returned!

At this writing, Roy is approaching his 11th (77th in dog years) birthday, but rather than acting like the senior citizen he is, he still behaves like a big loveable puppy, always happy to see his "grandma" (or anyone for that matter.) He loves to play in the snow or splash in the lake and will chase and fetch anything you throw for him. He has been on a diet and is weighing in at a svelte 95. He looks very handsome in his blue K.U. collar, a gentle giant of a dog.

40. THE ATTACK OF THE KILLER DACHSHUNDS

The next three years passed quickly. We were enjoying our empty nest and our two sweet pets. Our daughter had married and had two dachshunds (what else) of her own. Their registered names were Ham and Bean. When we went on one of our frequent trips, it was very convenient to just take Schnitz to her house. They didn't even need to be home; we just lifted him over the fence, and he went in through their doggy door and just melted into their household. This worked well until her husband took a job in New Jersey and they moved 1500 miles away!

It didn't take long for Mindy and her husband, Kent, to figure out that "the Big Apple" was too much for two Kansas kids, and they decided to come home. Mindy got a job in Overland Park first and moved back, while her husband (and the dogs) stayed to sell the house. After eight weeks of no offers, the realtor pointed out that the dogs were a deterrent to presenting the house's best features. In short, they had to go! Mindy flew to New Jersey and brought them back. When we met her at the airport, she came out carrying both of them in one carrier. They were wide-eyed and scared after four hours in the cargo hold!

We were not too excited about having two more four-legged guests, but since we had allowed Eric's cats, we couldn't refuse. Actually, they didn't disrupt the household too much. They slept with Mindy and we were there to take care of them during the day. I do remember one crisis when Ham slipped through the back fence. Larry and I and the carpenter working on our new deck all took off in opposite directions to search. The last thing I wanted to do was call Mindy at work and tell her we'd lost her 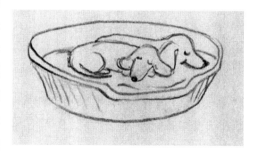 dog! We eventually found him in the church parking lot behind our property. We joked that Ham had gone to visit the Baptists!

All of our "weenie dogs" were barkers, yappy, vocal, little watch dogs. When the doorbell rang, all three would fly up or down the stairs, ears standing straight out, barking furiously. We called it the "attack of the killer dachshunds."

The three, all neutered males, had very different personalities. Bean was the fattest, and had very sad eyes. He had been hit by a car as a puppy and I think it affected him throughout his short (6-year) life. He was very loyal to his mistress and also very protective. One time when a utility man came to the door, Bean lunged out and bit him on the leg!

Ham was the most hyper, always jumping and running and barking. Schnitz, the oldest of the three was the most laid back, and, as previously mentioned, preferred to spend his time on my lap.

We attracted a lot of attention when we took the dogs for a walk. Mindy had a double leash for her two and of course, I would lead Schnitz. But often, they would see something of interest and all head for it at the same time, thus entangling the leashes and falling over each other like playful pups. If we saw another animal, they would bark loudly and in unison, and of course, go into their "tough guy" act. The goal of these outings was exercise for the dogs *and* us, but the cardio effects were minimal since we stopped every few steps for one or the other to mark his territory. The neighbors must have thought we were running a kennel!

That was a lively and memorable six months in our home. Eventually, the house in New Jersey sold, and the kids bought another house in Olathe and moved in (with their dogs) right before Christmas. They were settled in just in time to welcome our first grandchild!

41. THE SENIOR YEARS

By this time, Larry and I had celebrated our 40th anniversary, and were officially senior citizens, settling into a quieter lifestyle. We loved going out to movies and dinner or an evening of dominoes with good friends. Our pets were both seniors also, and were our constant and faithful companions. Larry had some problems during these years, but Schnitzel and Pouncer were blessed with good health, so we were very concerned when Pouncer suddenly became very lethargic and seemed to be losing weight.

We took him to the kind doctor who had cared for him since kittenhood. He told us the cat was diabetic, very weak and needed round-the-clock IVs. Since he had no night staff, he was unable to care for him. We rushed him to another vet (a close personal friend of Larry's brother) and he gave us the same diagnosis.

Frantically, we drove him to a 24-hour emergency clinic. After waiting nearly an hour, with a limp cat on my lap, I passed him off to my worried spouse and approached the desk. Ranting like a crazy person, I threatened to sue if the cat died while we were waiting to see a doctor. They called us in immediately.

Pouncer was in the hospital four days, while we waited anxiously for the doctor's calls, reporting on his progress. Upon release, his bill totaled nearly $2,000! This was quite an expenditure for a stray cat who was not even allowed out of the bedroom at one time; and the man who had hated cats didn't say a word! Isn't it amazing how one cream tabby can totally change a man's priorities!

We left with instructions to give him daily insulin injections. Only two months passed and we discovered a lump in his hindquarter. Our vet did an MRI and biopsy and gave us the bad news. It was cancer and it was inoperable. Refusing to accept this, we took him for a second opinion which confirmed it.

We took Pouncer home and loved him for another month, until one night we were awakened by him banging his head against our bedroom mirror. He was in obvious pain and we knew it was time. We sat and held him and cried until the vet opened and Larry took him in. Again, I couldn't face the end and chickened out. It's amazing that pets are with us such a short time in the span of our lives, and yet they can leave such a void when they're gone!

42. THE WILD ONE

Several "catless" months passed and Norma, one of my Tupperware dealers, called with a proposition. She was known in her neighborhood as the "cat lady" because she would round up strays, see that they were neutered and then find homes for them. Knowing we had lost Pouncer, she had found us a perfect pet. His name was "Pickle," after a character in a children's book. She extolled his virtues and assured me that all he needed was some TLC to convert him into a house cat.

We drove over to get him, and when he ran under the car and wouldn't come out, we should have taken that as an indication of what kind of pet he might make. We were not exactly experts on cat behavior, having owned only one in our combined lifetimes! We finally caught him and took him home, confining him to an upstairs bathroom. No one could approach him. If the door was opened, he would race around the room, leaping from the tub to the sink and climbing the shower curtain.

After a few days, we decided he needed more space and we moved him to the basement storage area, thinking he couldn't hurt anything there. What we failed to consider was that the open rafters gave him multiple places to hide! He immediately leaped upward and scurried over the finished ceiling of an adjoining room. And there he stayed! We tried everything to convince him to come down, including climbing on a ladder and extending a paddle with a tasty morsel of tuna on the end of it.

Our son, who had been intimately acquainted with several cats, came over and tried to extricate him. We also consulted some good friends who were cat-lovers. Of course, we called the veterinarian for his opinion. Nothing worked! His food dish and the litter box remained untouched. He wasn't even sneaking down at night!

Two weeks passed and Pickle never emerged from his hiding place. No one saw or heard him, but he had to be up there! *Didn't he?* Larry worried constantly about this critter over our ceiling, and as time went by, my concern was that he might die and begin to smell! I could see having to cut into the ceiling to retrieve the carcass!

Finally, Larry called Overland Park Animal Control. Surely they could help; after all, we'd been tax payers for forty years! Their response was they didn't deal with domestic animals, but they had traps for wild animals. We assured them that Pickle definitely fell into that category, so they brought us a trap and advised us to bait it with tuna. Amazingly enough, he came down the very first night and trapped himself! We immediately took him back to the "cat lady." She apologized for his behavior and theorized that he was a "ghetto cat" and couldn't adjust to the upscale Johnson County!

43. THE CUDDLE KITTY

After the Pickle debacle, you can imagine our reluctance to take on another stray when the cat lady called again. This one was only four months old and a female, a "real sweetheart." Larry refused to even consider another of Norma's projects. But she was very persistent in her efforts; seems she was convinced she had found the perfect pet for us. Finally she called when I was out and Larry answered the phone. Somehow, she persuaded him to just "look at this kitten." During the drive over, I remember him saying, "If this one doesn't like us immediately, we're NOT taking her home – none of this two week trial!"

When we arrived, this tiny gray fluff ball was nestled calmly in Norma's lap. She had been rescued from a dumpster at the school where Norma worked. We petted her, she purred convincingly, and in ten minutes, we were on our way. I held her, as we had been so sure we wouldn't want her that we hadn't taken a cat carrier with us! She grew restless on the long ride home and Larry said "Let her down. Let's see where she wants to go." We soon learned that where she wanted to go was onto Larry's shoulder, where she nuzzled his neck and purred all the way home. Smart cat!

We introduced her to her canine brother, Schnitz, who at age 15 (105 in dog years) could have cared less. She seemed to understand that he was harmless and didn't freak out at the sight of a dog. It didn't take long for us to decide that "Cuddles" was the most appropriate name we could think of. The vet estimated her age at five months, and after he spayed and declawed her, she was set to go!

She adjusted quickly to her new home, grateful, I'm sure, to be out of the dumpster. From the beginning, she was very social, welcoming guests at the door and purring against their legs. She would often jump on a lap, usually choosing the person who happened to be allergic to cats or who just didn't like them! If we didn't confine her in a bedroom, she would lay in the middle of the room, usually spread eagle on her back with all four paws extended. One of our friends dubbed her "slut kitty"; another commented that she seemed more like a dog.

She wore a collar and bell, and usually would come when called. We learned two things early on: she definitely had a unique personality and she liked men.

This was the last year we had two pets. It became increasingly difficult for Schnitz to go up and down the stairs. We had to carry him to the yard for his outings. When we were planning a trip to our lake house for Memorial Day weekend, we realized that he could no longer navigate the rough terrain down there. He had been a wonderful sweet pet, but it was time for us to let him go. It was especially hard this time because I think we both knew that he was our last dog. Since we were traveling a lot, it just wasn't practical to start over with a new puppy.

For the first time in our 45 years of marriage, we were dogless! Of course, we still had Cuddles.

44. THE ONE PET HOUSEHOLD

We learned quickly that life is easier in a one-pet household. We could leave Cuddles for two or three nights, and as long as she had plenty of sustenance and her litter box, she was fine. Of course, she was always a little annoyed with us when we returned, but her happiness in having us back seemed to overshadow her anger. If we took a longer trip, we had fellow cat lovers who periodically visited her for some play time.

However, when we decided to spend a whole month in Florida to escape the Kansas winter weather, there was no question that we had to find a place that was "pet friendly." We could never leave her for a month! When we found a house that sounded perfect except for the "no pets" clause, I called the owner to plead her case.

I explained that Cuddles was short-haired, declawed and had never had a litter box accident. I admit that we discussed "sneaking her in" but decided that honesty was the best policy. As it turned out, it was in this case, because the owner said she wouldn't be a problem.

45. TRAVELING WITH A CAT

Cuddles had inherited a pet carrier from her predecessor, Pouncer, and it was nearly unused because Pouncer refused to cram his sizeable girth into it and would splay out all four legs and "put on the brakes." Larry, therefore, assumed that Cuddles wouldn't like it either and declared that he was NOT going to make her ride that way for three days, so although I insisted on taking it along, it sat empty in the back of the van. It may have been used to hold cat food and toys, but never the cat!

Her litter box was placed strategically on the floor of the back seat, and after three miles of yowling protest, she settled down and slept on whichever lap was in the passenger seat. Occasionally, she'd sneak over to the driver's side or crawl up on Larry's shoulder. If we stopped for gas, she'd wake up and look out every window to check out the new surroundings. This never failed to draw amazed gasps from the other customers. We often noticed people pointing and saying, "Look! There's a cat in that car!" Apparently it's unusual to have a feline unsecured in a car!

The very first travel day, we were only 250 miles into the trip when we hit a piece of debris on the road, embedded it into a front tire and disabled our nearly new vehicle! We called the nearest Ford dealer and they sent a tow truck. The only problem was that state law prohibited anyone (any human that is) from riding in a car while being towed. We didn't mind riding in the tow truck, but Cuddles was not allowed! Two hours and one new tire later, we got back into the automobile and there was no sign of a cat! We eventually found her, huddled under the front seat, uncharacteristically frightened to death!

Traveling 1500 miles with a cat is a little like traveling with children, except that most motels will accept children as guests; pets are not quite so welcome. We had reservations at two hotels that allowed pets, and she was no problem. We carried her box in and placed it in the bathroom, and after sniffing every corner of the room, she would settle in for the night. Thus, the third night, even though the hotel said "no pets," we decided they would never know.

We failed to take into account how curious and friendly she is, and when Larry walked in with the cat safely zipped in his jacket, she heard voices and immediately poked her head out, looked around alertly and meowed loudly. It was if she had to announce her presence to everyone in the lobby. Larry kept walking and no one said a word!

Despite the hotel discrimination, there are some advantages to traveling with a cat instead of children. You don't have to worry about entertaining her for those long days in the car; there's no need to stop to use the bathroom and best of all, she never once asked, "Are we there yet?"

After three days of traveling, we arrived at our destination. Our rental was a three-bedroom house with a pool and a screened lanai. It was on one of the many inland canals in the Cape Coral area, so there was always wildlife and activity to watch. To a cat that's never been outside, this was a dream come true! She was safe because of the screen; but could watch all the birds and squirrels. She loved the little green lizards that abound in South

Florida and would chase them up the screen. I'm sure she would have been quite content to stay longer than our allotted 30 days.

The second year we went to Florida, we had a bigger house and bigger pool and yes, a bigger lanai. This pool had a robot cleaner that was on a timer and came on automatically each morning. The first day, I looked out and Cuddles was standing at the edge of the pool, intently staring at something in the water and moving her head in a circular motion. I immediately thought of all the stories I'd read about alligators getting into Florida pools. But instead, it was the pool robot! She continued to be fascinated by this and would run to the edge of the pool every time she heard it come on.

Cuddles had a special Florida neckerchief with a tropical scene on it. She wore this only while on vacation.

The second year we left Florida a day early to beat a predicted snow storm on the way home. We stayed ahead of it all through Georgia and into Tennessee. Finally, after 14 hours, we stopped in Paducah, Ky. We were tired and hungry and dressed in Florida clothes and it was 25 degrees and snowing! We stopped at the first likely looking motel and after Larry checked us in, we pulled behind the building to unload. There was a prominently displayed sign by the door saying "Absolutely NO pets" and promising a $100 fine.. We looked at each other and with the familiarity that comes with forty plus years of marriage, agreed to chance it. As luck would have it, our room was on the ground floor. The first thing Cuddles did was jump onto the window ledge, nose back the drapes and look out. We quickly ushered her into the bathroom where she protested her confinement with loud meows. We moved the radio in there to mask the noise. Neither of us got much sleep that night, and when morning finally arrived, I stood lookout, while Larry hustled the cat out to the car under his jacket. Maybe we just weren't cut out to be devious!

She did get busted the next year and we didn't even know it until the Visa bill arrived the next month. There was an extra $100 charge from a hotel in Ocala, Fla. When I called, they sent me a copy of the contract Larry had signed that said "no pets." Apparently he hadn't read the fine print or didn't have his bifocals! It seems the cleaning lady found kitty litter in the bathroom waste basket!

46. CUDDLES' NEW ROOM

Cuddles had enjoyed her screened play area so much, that when we returned home, we decided to screen in our upper deck and make a porch. It sounded so simple, and in theory, it was! In *reality,* we ended up having to tear off the existing deck, build a new one and then build a "screen room" atop that. To meet city requirements, a 30-inch panel was required up the side from the floor. This prevented the shortest member of the household (Cuddles) from looking out, and thus defeated the whole purpose of the project! We called the builders back out, applied for an exemption, and they were able to screen it all the way to the floor with just a board around the middle.

Five months and $15,000 later, Cuddles' new room was finished. It was worth the wait! She loves to be out there and clamors at the door to be allowed out. Our last Florida rental had sliding doors throughout the house, and she was used to going out at will. She is puzzled in the winter, however, when it's too cold. She seems to forget the temperature and insists on going out. Then she peers through the window at me, meowing to be let back in! I should add that her humans love the porch, too, although Larry only got to enjoy it one season.

47. CUDDLES AND ME

We both loved the Florida weather in the winter and the only thing stopping us from staying longer was the University of Kansas basketball schedule. Even though we joined the Florida Jayhawks to watch all the games, it just wasn't the same as actually being in old Allen Fieldhouse. Nevertheless, we made the difficult decision to relinquish our season tickets and spend two months in the south in 2009. We checked into flying, so we wouldn't have to deal with hotels to and from, but we couldn't find an airline that would allow us to take Cuddles, so of course, we decided to drive again. There was no other option!

As it turned out, all these plans were cancelled when the last week in September, Larry woke up with a sore throat one morning and by the next day, he was in the hospital in ICU. After two weeks, the last one on a respirator, he died on a beautiful Saturday morning in October.

After the services were held, and the out of town relatives left and everyone went home, Cuddles and I were left alone. The house seemed very quiet and very large, and I sat in Larry's big leather recliner, with the cat curled in my lap. If I cried, she'd purr and stand up and knead with her paws on my chest, as if she were saying, "It's okay, I'm still here."

The days stretched into weeks and I just concentrated on doing the things that had to be done: household chores, paying bills, winding up Larry's affairs. I also tried to stay busy with activities outside the house and even took several trips that winter. Every time I returned home, Cuddles would hear the garage door open and she'd be waiting in the hallway for me, usually with a vocal greeting. I learned to interpret her meows: a quiet one meant "welcome home," a loud frantic one, followed by a run to the kitchen meant, "I'm out of food!"

This year, when I took a long winter trip, I got a self-feeder for her, because even though I had lined up "Friends of Cuddles" to check on her, I was concerned that weather conditions might prevent them from their scheduled visits. When I returned from that trip and opened the door, I was startled to see what looked like a large grey porcupine sitting in the hallway. I think she had gained several pounds from her "all you can eat buffet!" Apparently, she had entertained herself by eating! Needless to say, I put her back on her measured portions twice a day!

48. THE SECOND FISH POND

We had been in our new home ten years when Larry retired and was ready for another fish pond project. This time, being older and wiser and a little wealthier, he decided to hire most of the work done, and consulted with The Water's Edge, a water garden supply merchant. After deciding on a location which had the required sun exposure and the shape and depth he wanted, he hired a strong back to hand-dig it. This done, he purchased a vinyl liner with a 30 year warranty to put in the hole. (Not taking a chance on leaks this time!) With great enthusiasm, he purchased water plants and joined the local Water Garden Society, and spent hours arranging his waterfall with just the right rocks and angle for the desired effect. Then it was time to stock the pond. He purchased several koi for color and then added assorted game fish. He even tried walleye pike, but quickly learned our Kansas temperatures in a shallow pond were too much for them!

We had a small catfish for several years and when he grew too large for the pond, Larry carefully fished him out with a barbless hook and carried him to a nearby lake. The other assorted bass, crappie and sunfish were hand-fed a fresh supply of minnows every two weeks. Talk about spoiled!

Larry thoroughly enjoyed his pond and spent hours of his retirement working on it. Once when we were out of town and heard that our home area had experienced torrential rain storms, Larry called the neighbor and asked him to make sure the pond hadn't overflowed. He had visions of the fish washing away!

Aside from helping him re-pot and fertilize the water lilies, I simply sat and enjoyed the pond and listened to the waterfall. In other words, I paid no attention to the almost daily maintenance. That was my spouse's department! Therefore, when he died and I suddenly inherited the pond duties, along with all the other yard chores, I had no clue as to how to proceed!

I had two choices. I could fill it in and plant a big flower garden in the spot, or I could try to care for it. The decision was clear to me: it had been so important to him that I had to try to maintain it in his memory. I made one concession. At my son's suggestion, I let him remove all the game fish, and take them to a lake so that I wouldn't have to deal with the bi-weekly minnow runs. The koi could just eat gold fish food.

There have been several challenges. Two weeks after Larry passed, I realized the leaves were falling and he always covered the pond to keep the debris out. The only problem was I didn't know where he stored the big net for this purpose. After calling several places, I finally located a 20 x 15-foot net, drove across town to buy it, and then, enlisted the help of two friends to stretch it over the water's surface.

The next challenge came with "winterizing." I did know that I had to trim the water lilies and then set them down on the bottom of the pond. My son helped me remove the waterfall pump and install a bubbler to keep the water from freezing over. It's amazing to me, but the fish simply hibernate in the bottom of the pond and then awaken when the water temperature reaches a certain point in the spring. I was thrilled that I didn't lose a single fish that winter!

One lovely spring morning I looked out the bedroom window and saw, standing by the fish pond, a long-legged bird. I had only seen these in Florida and other tropical locations. I called Eric and said, "Do we have herons in

Kansas?" His response was, "of course! He was probably just flying over, looked down and said, "lunch!" No way – not in my back yard!

When I researched this, I found that I could cover the pond with a net, or construct a 12-inch barricade around it. Either of these sounded very unattractive to me! I decided to take my chances, and as far as I know he hasn't been back. I was afraid he might tell all his bird friends about the new cafeteria he found!

The next problem occurred when I was sitting on the screened porch one day and suddenly realized something was wrong. I didn't hear that soothing running water from the waterfall. The pump had just stopped! In Larry's files, I was able to find the sales receipt and warranty. This was the good part. The bad part was, I had to drive it to Lawrence where he purchased it, to learn that the company had discontinued that model, and since Larry had bought it on sale a new one would cost an additional $100! Then I was faced with the problem of installing it. Somehow, I did it and we (rather, the waterfall) were up and running again!

I made it through that first summer with help from my son cleaning the filter; I repeated the whole winterizing process and into the next spring. So far, so good. It is now the Larry Myers Memorial Pond with a Jayhawk flag, a Navy insignia and two small American flags.

Time for another crisis! I looked out the window one day, and saw a flash of orange on the surface of the water. Why am I seeing the fish that clearly? They should be swimming underwater, I investigated and found one of the smaller koi was floating on his side. When I got the net and tried to fish him out, he breathed and swam away! Close call!

The next day, the same scenario. I'm no ichthyologist, but I do know that it is not a good sign when a fish lies on its side. My instinct said, get him out before he infects his pond mates, but he was still alive! When I called the Water's Edge, they verified that I should remove him, and said the "most humane way" was to put him in a zip-loc bag and stick him in the freezer.

I explained that I sell Tupperware – I don't buy zip-loc bags! (At least I resisted the temptation to launch into a sales presentation!) The confused salesclerk said, "Well, do you have any extra Tupperware you could put him in?" No problem! My son came over and quickly nabbed him to use as catfish bait!

It made me very sad to lose one of Larry's fish. I inexplicably felt I had let him down! So, my Mother's Day gift from Eric was five small koi in various colors.

They were quickly assimilated into the pond environment and I assume they're still there. At least I haven't found them floating on the top! When I go out to feed them, the larger fish surge to the top, grabbing the fish flakes as they filter down. Hopefully, the smaller ones are under there waiting for crumbs.

48. PSYCHO CAT

Larry had been gone several months when Cuddles developed some strange behavior. For the first time in her life, she was having "litter box issues." She would go on the floor (fortunately a concrete basement floor) about six inches from the box, then climb in the box and kick litter out, as if she were trying to cover it. She also started biting me, mainly on my ankles. This would occur if I was walking away from her. She would chase me and nip at my legs with her sharp little teeth. She also didn't like me to stand up if she was on my lap. If I had to answer the phone or go to the restroom, she'd become angry and lunge at my hand to bite it. If I scolded her or tried to punish her, she would become very combative and charge me.

I tried to empathize and think like a helpless animal, and I decided that she thinks I'm going to leave her, too.

That fateful night I had to call 911 for Larry, I locked her in the bathroom before the paramedics arrived, so she didn't even see him leave. In her mind, he disappeared and never came back! When I consulted with her vet, he said it was "stress" and put her on kitty Prozac.

Although I felt guilty drugging her, the sedative alleviated the situation somewhat. At least she started using her litter box again and the bites are less frequent. She still insists on climbing onto the table. It's difficult in the morning to drink coffee and read my paper, because she's there nudging me and batting the paper. Occasionally she even sticks a paw into my coffee cup! It's pretty obvious who's in charge here, and it's not me, but the little grey shadow that follows me everywhere!

A friend recently noticed the scabs around my ankle and on my hand and commented that he knew what he'd do to that cat! Others have asked why I put up with her? I guess the answer is that when she jumps into my lap and curls up and purrs, her companionship and loyalty is all worth it! We've been through a lot together and now, she's my "immediate" family!

Hopefully we'll have many more years together!

LaVergne, TN USA
19 November 2010
205645LV00002B/1/P